Contents

Getting started

All you need to start drawing animals is a pencil and some paper. Look at animals all around you – in real life, wildlife films, photographs, books or on the internet – for inspiration. Here are some ideas of things to do to get started.

Drawing and collecting

Artists keep sketchbooks which they fill with lots of drawings, ideas and information. Keep a folder and fill it with drawings, photographs and pictures of animals to use as reference.

Make quick drawings of animals around you.

Keep unfinished sketches to use as reference.

Collect photographs of wild animals or pets.

Usborne **ART** ideas

DRAWING ANIMALS

Anna Milbourne

Designed and illustrated by Jan McCafferty,
Doriana Berkovic, Nickey Butler and Non Figg

Consultant: Gill Figg

Additional illustrations by Catherine-Anne MacKinnon, Gill Figg,
Anna Milbourne, Cristina Adami, Fiona Watt and Christyan Fox
Cover design by Sarah Vince
Photographs by Howard Allman
Image manipulation by John Russell

Usborne Quicklinks

At the Usborne Quicklinks website we've provided links to websites and video clips with lots more inspiration and tips for drawing animals, plus downloadable pictures from this book.

Discover online

Throughout this book you'll see boxes with QR codes, like this one.

Scan the codes with a smartphone or tablet to watch video clips of animals, follow online drawing lessons, find tips on art techniques and lots more.

Links to all the video clips are also available at the Usborne Quicklinks website along with lots more recommended websites and the downloadable pictures from this book.

To visit Usborne Quicklinks go to www.usborne.com/quicklinks and enter the keywords "drawing animals".

Downloadable pictures

The pictures marked with a * in this book can be downloaded from the Usborne Quicklinks website. You can use the pictures in your art projects at home or at school, but they may not be used online or for commercial purposes.

Staying safe online

Please read our internet safety guidelines at the Usborne Quicklinks website. For more advice on using the internet and scanning QR codes, see the help and advice pages at the Usborne Quicklinks website.

1515
RHINOCERVS

Do simple drawings to capture an animal's pose.

Try out materials to get different effects.

Buy postcards of famous paintings from art galleries and shops.

Materials

Various materials were used to draw and paint the animals in this book. These are explained as you come across them.

Find out how to draw an orangutan using chalk pastels on pages 22-23.

Find out how to draw cats using felt-tip pen and watercolours on pages 36-37.

Find out how to paint this panda using a brush and ink on pages 30-31.

Discover online
Scan the code to see animals to draw.

For more links, go to
www.usborne.com/quicklinks

Animal outlines

A good way of looking at animals' shapes is by copying their outlines from photos. Try drawing outlines of animals onto black paper to make shadowy shapes. You can get different effects by drawing onto patterned paper.

The silver paper looks like moonlight shining on the fox's tail.

Fox in the moonlight

1. Find a simple picture of an animal to copy. Side views of animals tend to make good, recognizable outlines.

2. Start copying the animal's outline onto black paper. If you make a mistake, don't rub it out, just draw a new line.

3. As you draw, check that the proportions are right. For example, this fox's body is three times as long as its head.

4. At the same time, check which parts of the fox's body line up with each other. This will help get the shape right.

5. When you have finished drawing the outline, cut the shape out. Rub out any pencil lines that are left.

6. Lay the fox on some silver foil. Draw around the tip of its tail. Cut this shape out and glue it onto the fox's tail.

Silver paper was added to these animal shapes to make a moonlit scene.

More animal shapes

Try using patterned paper to make animal shapes. You can sometimes find pages in magazines that look like fur or skin, or you could paint paper to look like animal patterns.

Discover online

Scan the code to look at animals' shapes and copy outlines from photos.

For more links, go to **www.usborne.com/quicklinks**

Reptiles have geometrically shaped scales.

Giraffes have evenly spaced splodges.

Leopards have spots with black outlines.

7

Seeing shapes

Animals may look complicated to draw because they are all different shapes. You can draw animals more easily if you break them down into simpler shapes, such as circles and triangles. Here are some examples.

Discover online

Scan the code to find out how to draw a cheetah by starting with simple shapes.

For more links, go to
www.usborne.com/quicklinks

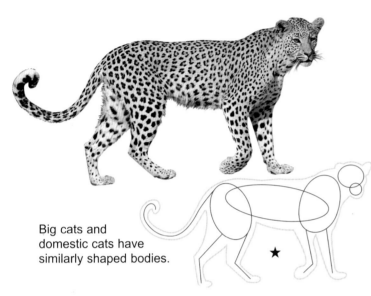

Big cats and domestic cats have similarly shaped bodies.

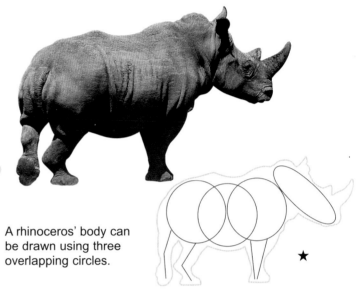

A rhinoceros' body can be drawn using three overlapping circles.

A penguin's body can be drawn using one oval.

A crocodile's jaws can be drawn using overlapping triangles.

A marmot's body can be drawn using ovals and circles.

An antelope's body can be drawn using overlapping ovals.

8

Running dog

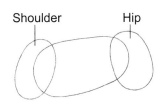

Shoulder   Hip

1. In pencil, lightly draw a slanted oval body, with an oval on either side for the hip and the shoulder.

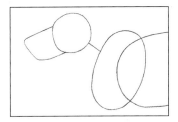

2. Draw the neck as a line coming from the shoulder. Add a circle for the head. Then, add the snout.

These legs are partly hidden.

3. Draw lines to position the legs. Add small circles for leg joints and paws. Two legs are partly hidden.

★

Draw this leg last.

4. Pressing quite lightly, draw an outline around the shapes using smooth, curving lines.

Hip

5. Draw a tail. The tail is a continuation of the backbone, so make it flow from the top of the hip.

Bend the line where the ear meets the head.

6. Add the ear, starting from the head circle. Then, rub out all the shapes inside the outline.

7. Draw the eye. Fill it in, leaving a white circle for a highlight. Fill in the nose, also leaving a highlight.

Add little dots near the nose.

8. Add little lines for fur around the dog's outline. Add patches by filling areas with lots of little lines.

The lines in each patch flow in the same direction.

Some white paper was left showing for a sheen along the dog's back.

A grey pencil was used to add the shadow beneath the dog.

Computer birds

Computers with Microsoft® Windows® have a program called Paint which you can use for drawing. (Page 58 tells you how to open it.) Paint has shape-drawing tools which can help you to draw animals.

Tools and colours

Along the left side of the Paint window, there is a tool box. To draw, you first need to choose a tool. To do this, move your pointer over the tool and click with the left mouse button.

The tool box

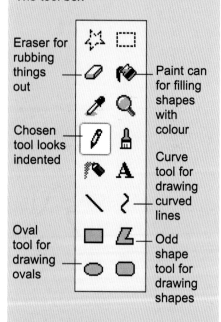

Eraser for rubbing things out

Paint can for filling shapes with colour

Chosen tool looks indented

Curve tool for drawing curved lines

Oval tool for drawing ovals

Odd shape tool for drawing shapes

There is a paint box at the bottom of the Paint window in which you can choose a colour to use. To do this, move your pointer over a coloured square and click.

The paint box

This box shows the colour you have chosen.

Drawing ovals

To draw an oval, start with the pointer here.

Drag the pointer to here.

Click on the oval tool. Hold the left mouse button down and move the mouse. This is called dragging. Let go of the mouse button to finish the oval.

Curvy lines

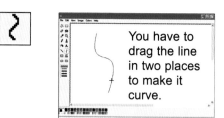

You have to drag the line in two places to make it curve.

Click on the curve tool. Hold the left mouse button down, drag, and let go. Put the pointer on the line and drag it into a curve. Drag it again.

Rubbing out

You can rub things out with the eraser tool. Click on the tool, then hold the left mouse button down and drag the pointer over whatever you want to rub out.

Filling in

Make sure the tip of the paint drip is inside the shape.

The shape must have an unbroken outline, or the colour will leak out.

To fill a shape with colour, click on the paint can tool, and then on a colour in the paint box. Move the paint can over the shape and click to fill it in.

Odd shapes

You can draw as many sides as you like.

Click on the odd shape tool. Hold the left mouse button down and drag the mouse to draw a side. Let go of the button, then press and drag to make the next side. Double-click to finish the shape.

Draw these shapes quite big.

Fill in each oval with the paint can as you go.

1. Click on blue, then on the oval tool. Draw an oval body and a smaller oval head above it. Fill them in with blue.

2. Use the curve tool to draw two curved lines for the neck, connecting the body to the head. Fill in the neck with blue.

3. For the eye, draw a white oval. Add a blue one inside it and a black one inside that. Do a tiny white oval for a highlight.

Make sure there are no gaps before filling the feathers.

Add a wing shape using the curve tool.

4. Click on orange. Use the odd shape tool to draw a beak and two legs. Use the paint can to fill them in.

5. Use the curve tool to draw one side of a feather. Draw another curve for the other side. Fill them with orange.

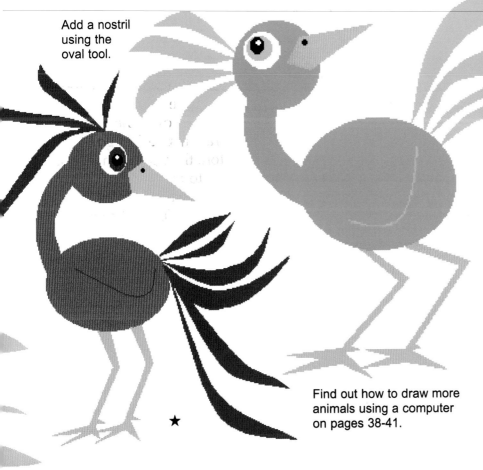

Add a nostril using the oval tool.

Find out how to draw more animals using a computer on pages 38-41.

Find out how to draw more animals using a computer on pages 38-41.

Discover online
To see lots of pictures of birds, go to
www.usborne.com/quicklinks

Making mistakes

If you make a mistake, hold the CTRL key down and press Z. To get rid of everything on your page, hold the CTRL key down, press N, then click on *No* in the box that appears.

11

Inside and out

It helps to understand a bit about what animals' insides look like, to be able to draw their outsides. Although animals all look so different, there are similarities in the way their bodies work. There are also a couple of tricks that can help you work out their shapes.

On this drawing of a cow (from 'Three cows') by Pisanello, you can see where its bones stick out, especially along the spine.

Animals and people

There are similarities between a four-legged animal's skeleton and a person's skeleton. Comparing the two can help you work out which way animals bend their legs.

This man is on all fours, so that you can see the similarities between his skeleton and the cow's.

The cow skeleton has the same labels as the man, so that you can compare their joints.

Zigzag legs

A handy trick for drawing animals' legs is to imagine a zigzag shape inside them. Most four-legged animals have a zigzag leg shape. There's more about zigzag legs on page 48.

The zigzags show where the bones are.

The zigzags are different shapes in different poses.

Bony cow

Press quite lightly.

1. In pencil, draw a straight line for the spine, with a big oval near each end for the shoulder and hip bones.

Make the front leg quite straight.

Ribcage

2. Add a curved line between the ovals for the ribcage. Add zigzag legs with circle joints from the shoulder and the hip.

3. For the head, do a rounded triangle, and a circle. The spine is a bit higher than the middle of the triangle.

The hooves slant forward.

4. Draw an outline around the shapes, like the one above. Draw the tail, making it flow from the cow's back.

5. You can only see part of the cow's other legs. Draw leg lines with circle joints on them first, then draw their outlines.

6. Rub out the extra lines. Add an udder. Draw an ear, horns and nostril. Add an eye. Fill it in, leaving a white dot inside it.

The background was filled in using coloured pencils.

Patches were added to this cow using black coloured pencil.

Discover online

Scan the code to see some animals' skeletons.

For more links, go to
www.usborne.com/quicklinks

White parts were left on the hooves to show highlights.

Light and dark

Adding areas of light and dark, or shading, can help to make your drawing look solid and three-dimensional. This section shows two different ways of shading, using pencil and ink.

Light and shape

When light shines on something, the parts facing the light are palest; the parts facing away from the light are darkest. By adding light, medium and dark areas, you can make a drawing look solid.

The light is coming from here.

Darkest area

Medium area

Lightest area

The snails' shadows fall away from the light.

Smooth blend seal

Rub out the lines that overlap the flippers and tail.

Add lines to the flippers on the end of the tail.

Add dark shading under the body and on the back and the tail.

1. Draw a seal shape as shown above. Start with the big teardrop body and then add the flippers, tail and face.

2. Shade the body by pressing lightly with a pencil and filling the shape in. Leave the lightest areas white.

3. Go over the areas you want to be dark, pressing harder. Press lighter as you reach the medium areas to blend the two.

Ink-wash fish

Paint as many bodies as you like.

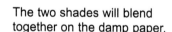

The two shades will blend together on the damp paper.

1. In a saucer, mix blue ink with lots of water to make a pale shade. Then, paint the oval bodies of the fish.

14

2. Add more ink to the saucer, and, while the fish bodies are still damp, paint the darker shade on their undersides.

3. When the fish are totally dry, use a blue fountain pen or felt-tip pen to draw their outlines, faces and scales.

Discover online
Scan the code to watch
a video clip about shading.

For more links, go to
www.usborne.com/quicklinks

These seals were
painted in exactly
the same way as
the ink-wash fish.

In this scene, the sea
was painted first, and
left to dry. Then, the
seals and fish were
added. See pages
54-55 for more about
backgrounds.

Fur and wrinkles

Animals have all sorts of different textures, from shaggy fur to wrinkly skin. As you are shading an animal, there are various ways in which to draw its fur, feathers, skin or scales.

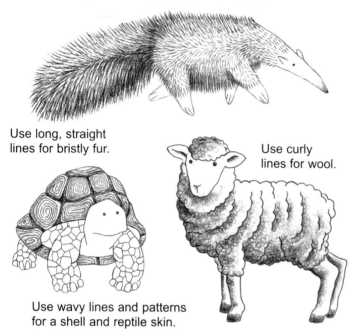

Use long, straight lines for bristly fur.

Use curly lines for wool.

Use wavy lines and patterns for a shell and reptile skin.

In his painting, 'A Young Hare', Albrecht Dürer uses lots of paintbrush strokes to show the texture of the animal's fur.

Furry mouse

The teardrop should tilt upwards.

1. Pressing very lightly with a pencil, draw a teardrop shape for the mouse's body. Then, add ears, an eye and the tail.

Adding less texture in the light parts and more in the dark parts shows the animal's shape.

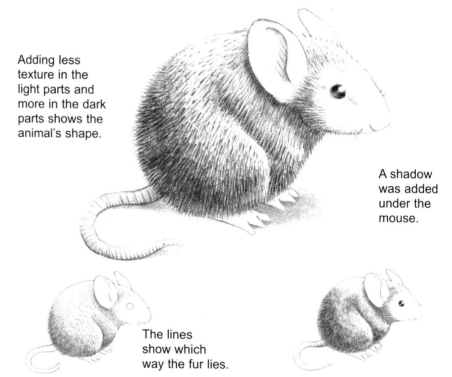

A shadow was added under the mouse.

Rub out this extra line.

2. Add a curve inside the teardrop shape for the head. Draw a curve for the back leg and draw two little feet.

The lines show which way the fur lies.

3. Do lots of tiny lines on the body. Do more lines to make darker areas. Leave the lightest areas white.

4. Using a dark pencil, do lines in the darkest areas. Add lines on the tail. Colour the mouse's eye black, but leave a highlight.

16

Wrinkly elephant

1. Using pencil, draw an oval body and a smaller oval head. Draw zigzag leg lines with circles for joints. Add oval feet.

When the paper is dry, you may have to re-draw parts of the outline if the water has washed it away.

The trunk curls back and touches the head.

2. Add a triangular ear. Draw two lines for the trunk curling up into the air. Add a line for the tail.

The watery ink shows the elephant's shape and the pen lines show its wrinkles.

Discover online
Scan the code for photos of elephants to inspire your drawings.

For more links, go to
www.usborne.com/quicklinks

3. Draw the outline in water-soluble felt-tip pen. Add an eye. Then, rub out the pencil lines.

4. Wet a paintbrush and paint water under the elephant's belly, touching the outline. The ink will spread.

5. Paint touches of water elsewhere on the elephant, spreading the colour to shade the body.

6. Let the drawing dry. Then, draw lines to show wrinkles. Do curves around the knees and trunk.

17

Patterned owl

One good way of drawing animal textures is to simplify them into patterns. This can have a dramatic effect. Varying the thickness of the line you use can add to the effect. Use a thin and a thick felt-tip pen to draw this owl.

This shows how you can draw different patterns to show feathers either realistically or in a simplified style.

Short lines or zigzags show feathers around the eyes.

Breast feathers are shorter and rounder like this.

Rows of dashes show head feathers.

Wing feathers are leaf shapes with lines inside them.

This painting 'Roosters' by Ito Jakuchu shows how simple patterns can be used to show lots of different types of feathers.

The body is twice as long as the head.

1. Draw a slanted oval for the owl's body, and another oval for its head. Add wing shapes. Then add clawed feet.

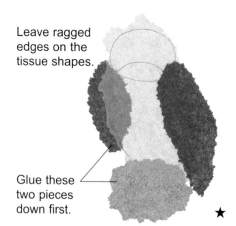

Leave ragged edges on the tissue shapes.

Glue these two pieces down first.

2. Using tissue paper, tear out a shape for the head and body, two wings and a tree stump. Glue them onto the drawing.

3. With a black felt-tip pen, draw the beak, tufts and eyes. Fill them in. Do lines across the head in thin and thick felt-tip.

18

Curve the dashes around the feet.

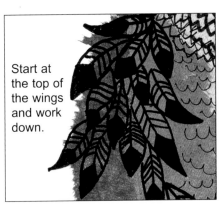

Start at the top of the wings and work down.

4. Using a thin and a thick felt-tip pen, do zigzag lines around the eyes. Add slanted lines and nostrils on the beak.

5. Draw downy breast feathers with curved lines in thin and thick felt-tip pen. Outline the feet and draw dashes on them.

6. Use thick felt-tip pen to fill the wing shapes with long feathers. Add lines to them and fill in the tips.

Patterns curving around the head and breast show the owl's shape.

This moon was torn out of tissue paper.

Different patterns on different areas of the owl show the various textures of its feathers.

Discover online

Scan the code to see an owl close up.

For more links, go to **www.usborne.com/quicklinks**

Chalky polar bears

You can draw these polar bears using chalk pastels to get a soft, furry effect. The bears' white fur and their snowy surroundings mean you only need black and white chalk pastels to create the picture. Chalk pastels are crumbly and smudgy, but easy to use.

Discover online

Scan the code for a video about chalk pastels.

For more links, go to
www.usborne.com/quicklinks

Chalk pastels work well on coloured paper.

Leave room for another bear on the right.

1. With a white chalk pastel, press lightly and draw shapes like these for the first polar bear. Draw them quite big.

The neck slopes down here.

Take care around the overlapping nose.

2. To the right of the first bear, draw the shapes for the second one. Make its nose overlap the first bear.

3. Draw the bears' outlines around the shapes with smooth, curved lines. Add arches for their legs.

4. Use a small piece of black chalk pastel on its side to fill in some dark areas on the two polar bears, like this.

Rest your hand on a scrap of paper to avoid smudging your picture as you draw.

5. Use a white chalk pastel on its side to colour the light areas. Go right up to the black parts with the white colour.

6. Using your finger, gently smudge the black and white together where they meet. The smudged bit will go grey.

7. To show the bears' fur, do short, slanted lines in black all over the grey areas, and also around the black edges.

Go round the ears in white.

8. In white, do more slanted lines in the grey areas and also around the white edges, to show the fluffy white fur.

9. Do a little black mark for each eye and semicircles for the ears. Colour the tips of the noses in black.

10. Draw some hills in black and white. Add shadows under the bears' feet. Blend them gently with your finger.

Blue paper helps the scene look icy and cold.

You will need to fix your drawing so that it won't smudge. See page 59 for how to do this.

Hairy orangutan

Chalk pastels can be used to show different kinds of texture. For example, you can blend two or three colours together to show an orangutan's skin, and you can use unblended lines to show the long hair on its body.

Draw in the middle of the paper. Press lightly to make pale lines.

The circles line up diagonally.

1. With an orange chalk pastel, draw three circles on green paper, as shown here.

Hand

Elbow

Shoulder

Snout

This elbow lines up with the middle of the biggest circle.

2. Add a circle for the snout. Draw lines for arms, then add circular joints and oval hands.

3. Draw two bent lines for legs. Then, add circular knees and oval feet.

★ Add a branch in brown pastel.

These fingers curl around the branch.

4. Draw the outline, like this, going around the arms and legs. Add fingers and toes.

Blow on the paper to get rid of any pastel dust.

5. With a pale orange pastel, fill in these areas. Blend them in with your finger.

Smudge the dark areas to the edges of the light ones.

6. Fill in the dark areas with a brown pastel. Blend them in with your finger.

7. Add hair with orange and brown pastels. Use long lines and don't blend them.

8. Add a little pink on the face, chest and belly and blend it in with your finger.

Try drawing a line of swinging orangutans.

Draw a pale line along the top of the branch for a highlight.

The fingers and toes were outlined with the tip of a black pastel.

9. Add some pale pink lines for highlights on the arms, face, legs, and feet.

You need to fix your picture so it doesn't smudge. See page 59 for how to do this.

10. With a black pastel, draw eyes and nostrils. Draw a line for the mouth and add the ear.

Discover online

Scan the code to watch a video clip about orangutans.

For more links, go to
www.usborne.com/quicklinks

23

Mixing colours

The animal world is full of colour, from bright parrots to patterned tabby cats. Knowing how to mix different colours will help you make the most of animals' colours in your drawings.

Discover online

Scan the code to watch a video about mixing colours.

For more links, go to
www.usborne.com/quicklinks

Bare necessities

There are three basic colours which you cannot make by mixing other colours: red, yellow and blue. These are called primary colours. Using these three colours, you can mix almost any other colour you will need.

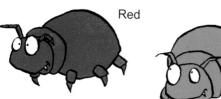

Red   Blue   Yellow

All mixed up

By mixing primary colours together you can make more colours: orange, green and purple. These are secondary colours. By altering how much of each colour you use in the mix, you can make different shades of these colours.

The beak on the toucan above was painted mixing red and yellow together to make shades of orange.

The circle is a colour wheel. It shows how colours are related to one another.

★

Yellow and red at either end of this snake mix to make shades of orange.

Blue and yellow at either end of this snake mix to make shades of green.

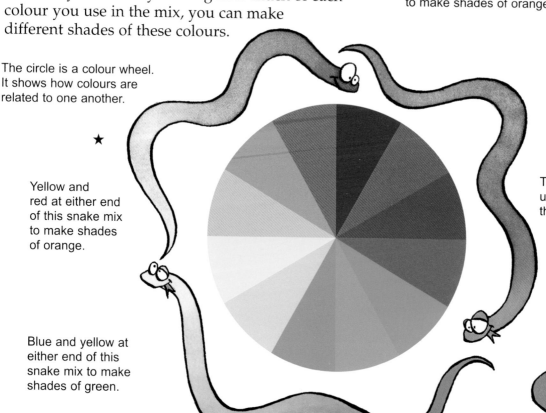

Red and blue at either end of this snake mix to make shades of purple.

This snake was painted using all the colours on the colour wheel.

★

A relaxed chameleon is the same colour as its surroundings. This helps it to hide.

This red poison arrow frog stands out against the green leaves.

Blending in

Some animals have colours which blend in with their surroundings. Use colours next to each other on the colour wheel to show this.

Showing off

Some animals have colours which stand out against their surroundings. Use colours from opposite sides of the colour wheel, such as red and green, to show this. These colours look brighter when next to each other.

Mixing shades

If you mix all three primary colours together, they make neutral colours like brown. Start with a mixture of two primary colours and add the third bit by bit to mix these shades.

Mix red and yellow.

Add a dab of blue.

Add more blue.

Add more blue.

Mix blue and yellow.

Add a dab of red.

Add more red.

Add more red.

Mix blue and red.

Add a dab of yellow.

Add more yellow.

Add more yellow.

Lighter and darker

If you add white to colours you can make them lighter. You can make colours darker by adding black, but this also makes them duller. Sometimes adding another colour, such as blue, can work better.

This armadillo was painted brown.

White was added to the brown to make this colour.

Blue was added to the brown to make this colour.

Painted parrot

To paint this parrot you only need paints in the primary colours: red, yellow and blue. All the other colours can be mixed from these. This picture can be painted with poster paints or acrylics.

Discover online

Scan the code to see lots more parrots to paint.

For more links, go to **www.usborne.com/quicklinks**

Acrylics and poster paints

Poster paints and acrylics are both good for painting solid areas of colour. Here are some tips on how to use them.

Use your brush to dab some of the paint onto a saucer. Mix water into the paint to make it runnier and easier to paint with.

Rinse your brush well before using another colour.

Don't let the paint dry on your brush, or it will ruin the bristles.

To mix a new colour, first put dabs of the colours you are mixing onto a plate. Mix the paints together in the middle of the plate, little by little, until you get the colour you want.

Once acrylic or poster paint is dry, you can paint on top of it with another colour.

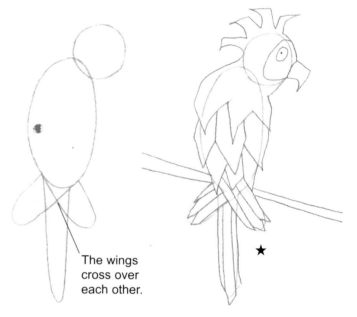

The wings cross over each other.

1. Using a pencil, draw a big oval for the body, and a circle for the head. Then, add the wing and tail feathers.

2. Join the shapes up like this. Draw big, jagged feathers. Add a beak, an eye and a perch.

3. Mix a drop of water into some red paint and paint the parrot's head and tail feathers. Let them dry.

4. Rinse your brush and paint the yellow feathers. Let them dry. Rinse your brush and paint the blue feathers.

The black outline is thicker in some places than others.

More colours were mixed to paint these flowers and leaves.

5. Mix a little yellow with the same amount of red to make orange. Paint the orange feathers.

6. Rinse your brush. Mix a little blue and the same amount of yellow to make green. Paint the last feathers.

7. Mix a small amount of yellow, blue and red together to make brown. Paint the parrot's perch.

8. Mix yellow with water to make it pale. Paint the beak and face. When it's dry, paint a brown eye.

9. Leave the painting to dry. Then, go round the outlines of your parrot with a black felt-tip pen.

27

Hunting tiger

Many animals have patterned coats, so that they can either hide or hunt without being seen. The background of a drawing can emphasize this. Using different shades of the same colours for the animal and its surroundings helps the animal blend in. See page 25 for tips on mixing different shades.

In his painting 'Tiger in a Tropical Storm (Surprised!)', Henri Rousseau uses shapes and colours to help the tiger blend in.

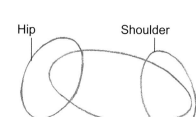

Hip   Shoulder

The long oval slants down to the right.

1. Draw a long oval for the tiger's body. Add another two ovals overlapping it for the hip and shoulder.

2. Add a circle for the head. It should be halfway down the shoulder oval. Add a small oval muzzle.

3. Draw zigzag lines for the legs with circles for joints. Draw a line for the tail from the top of the hip oval.

Add an ear far back on the tiger's head.

★

Look at the main picture to see where to put the white parts.

4. Draw the tiger's outline. Rub out the extra lines inside the outline, and then draw lines to show the white parts.

5. Draw a grass shape behind the tiger. Add blades of long grass overlapping the tiger and leaves in the foreground.

You can let the green paint overlap the grass stems slightly.

6. Mix some green paint and paint the background. Use watery green to paint the area below the tiger. Let it dry.

Discover online
To see lots of pictures of tigers, go to,**www.usborne.com/quicklinks**

7. Mix orange using red and yellow paint. Paint the tiger. Paint its belly and the flashes on its head white.

8. When the tiger is dry, paint its stripes in dark brown. Paint the tiger's eye, nose and mouth in black.

9. Mix a range of different greens and browns (see page 25). Paint simple grass and leaf shapes in different shades.

This tiger was painted using acrylic paints.

Details on the leaves and grass were added in brown and green.

Inky panda

You can use a brush and ink to do simple paintings of animals. Using watery and strong shades of two colours can give a striking effect. Use a soft brush with a pointed tip for this type of picture.

Using inks

Coloured inks come in bottles or cartridges. You can cut off the end of a cartridge and squeeze the ink onto a saucer.

Use ink straight from the bottle or cartridge for a strong shade.

Dab lots of water onto a saucer, then dab a little ink into it to mix a pale shade.

Ink is very runny. Dip your brush in the ink, then dab it on a paper towel before painting, so it doesn't drip.

Rinse your brush well and dry it before using a different colour.

1. Mix watery black ink. Paint the panda's head and body, using a smooth, flowing line. Leave it to dry.

3. Use undiluted black ink on the very tip of your brush to paint little, round eyes and a nose. Leave them to dry.

Make the paws shaggy around the edges.

2. Use undiluted black ink to paint the ears. Paint a stripe over the chest, then add the arms and legs. Let them dry.

The patches slope outwards at the bottom.

4. Paint the panda's eye patches in undiluted black ink. Leave a little white circle around each eye.

Bamboo

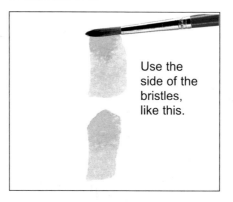

Use the side of the bristles, like this.

1. Mix watery green ink and paint a section of bamboo stem. Paint sections above it, leaving gaps between them.

Let the stems dry before adding the leaves in undiluted ink.

2. Use one brush stroke for each leaf. Press lightly with the tip of the brush, then press harder, and then lightly again.

The joints
on the stems
were painted
in undiluted
ink when
the stems
were dry.

The grass was
painted in the same
way as the leaves.

31

Watercolour giraffe

Painting tips

Watercolour paints come in either tubes, or blocks called pans. Here are some tips on using them.

With pans, rub a wet brush on the pan to get paint on the bristles. Dab the paint onto a saucer.

With tubes, squeeze a tiny blob from the tube onto a saucer, and add water with your brush.

Add more water to make the colour paler.

Wet watercolours blur together.

Let a colour dry before adding the next one if you don't want them to blur.

Watercolour paints are good for adding colour to drawings without hiding the original outline. If you want to draw the outline of an animal before painting it, you need to use a permanent pen – one which doesn't run when it gets wet.

1. Start near the top of the paper. In pencil, draw two circles for the head and muzzle and two long lines for the neck.

2. Draw a triangular body with an oval hip. Add four long stick legs. Put circles halfway down the front legs.

3. Draw the giraffe's outline in permanent pen. Make the knees knobbly. Add the hooves, a mane and a tail.

4. Add ears, horns, eyes with semi-circular eyelids, and curly nostrils. Then, rub out the pencil lines.

Don't worry about it being neat.

5. Draw a low hill and a tree. Mix yellow watercolour with a little red and fill in the giraffe's shape.

The orange splodges will blur on the damp paper.

6. Mix a bright orange. Dab splodges all over the giraffe's body while the paper is still damp.

7. Paint the mane and tail orange, and the hooves and horns grey. Dampen the background a little and paint it. Let the colours blur together.

When the paint is dry, you could add a pen line around the picture to frame it.

See pages 54-55 for tips on painting backgrounds.

Discover online

Scan the code to watch a video about painting with watercolours.

For more links, go to
www.usborne.com/quicklinks

You can do all kinds of animals using this technique. Draw quickly. If the lines are a little lopsided it gives the animal more character.

The blurry effect can add to the picture. Here, the pink from the flamingo has spread into the water and looks like a reflection.

Paint a very simple background to make the animal stand out.

33

Watercolour dolphins

When painting with watercolours, you can build up colour gradually in layers, or washes. You can get different effects by painting onto wet or dry paper. It's best to use watercolour paper (see page 59) for this dolphin picture, but if you don't have any, you can use thick cartridge paper instead.

Painting washes

Here is how to paint a wash:

1. Wet a sponge and wipe it evenly across your paper to make it damp.

You could use a small dish to mix the wash in.

2. Mix lots of water and a colour together to make a pale shade.

Overlap the brush strokes for an even wash.

3. Using a big brush, paint the wash in overlapping strokes onto the paper.

Two colours blend together on damp paper.

4. To add another colour or shade to the wash, paint it onto the damp paper.

Painting on rough watercolour paper gives a grainy effect, like this.

1. Pressing lightly, draw three curved teardrop shapes in blue pencil. Then, add the dolphins' beaks and fins.

2. Draw the water and a few droplets. Draw one dolphin's tail. The other tails are hidden. Add their flippers and eyes.

Discover online
Scan the code to see some different techniques for watercolour washes.

For more links, go to
www.usborne.com/quicklinks

Paint the water droplets in blue, like the sea.

Waves painted on damp paper have soft, blurry edges.

A shape painted on dry paper has clear, sharp edges.

The blue will blend in with the green on the damp bodies.

3. Paint a pale green wash over the paper. Then, add blue waves to the sea while the paper is damp. Let it dry.

4. Mix blue, a little yellow and lots of water to make a blue-green wash. Fill in each dolphin with the wash.

5. Mix blue paint with water, and paint the tops of the damp bodies. Let them dry. Add the eyes and mouths in black pencil.

35

Character cats

Cartoonists and illustrators have drawn animals in various ways, often giving them amusing characters. The scene below was created by drawing lots of cats, all with different expressions.

1. Using watercolour paints, mix a watery orange colour. Paint an oval body. It needn't be too neat.

2. Mix a brighter shade of orange for some stripes. Paint them while the paper is still a bit damp.

3. When the cat is dry, draw an outline in fine felt-tip pen. Add lines for the front legs and oval paws with claws.

4. Draw a face, some whiskers and a tail. Draw quickly – it adds character if it's a bit lopsided.

Expressions

By changing the size, shape and the faces on the cats you can give them different characters. Here are a few ideas.

Caterwauling cats have closed eyes high on their heads and open mouths.

A fat cat has a small, high face.

A scared cat has circles with dots in them for eyes.

A cross cat has slanted lines above its eyes.

Edward Lear, an artist and an author of nonsense poetry, drew his cat, Foss, in all sorts of comical poses. Here are three examples.

Foss, a untin.

Foss dansant

Foss rampant

Discover online
Scan the code to see how to draw a cheetah by starting with simple shapes.

For more links, go to www.usborne.com/quicklinks

The watercolour background was painted before the cats for this scene. See page 55 for how to do backgrounds.

Grey shapes were painted for bins, and then the outlines and details were added in pen.

Computer camels

The computer program Paint has tools which enable you to draw an animal and then copy it again and again. (To open Paint, see page 58). You can find out how to use the brush tool below, but look at page 10 for how to use the other tools you'll need to draw these camels.

Drawing an outline

To draw, click on the brush tool. Click on a brush style in the options (see below) to choose a type of line to use. Position the pointer over the white screen, hold the left mouse button down and drag the mouse.

Brush tool

When you click on the brush tool, these options appear below the tool box.

The camels were drawn using this brush style.

Camel train

Don't draw the head too big.

Make sure the outline has no gaps in it.

1. Click on a small brush style. Draw the camel's ears and nose. Add the jaw. Then, draw two curves for the neck.

2. Add an eye and nostril. Draw two humps. Draw the top side of the tail up to the tip. Then, add the rest of the tail.

3. Draw the front leg – first draw the part from the neck to the middle of the toes, then the rest. Add the belly.

★

4. Draw the back leg. Then, add the other two legs under the belly. Make sure there are no gaps in the outline.

You'll need to rub out this line.

5. Draw reins and patterns on the humps. Click on the eraser tool. Rub out the line where the reins overlap the body.

Start the rectangle here.

A dotted line will appear.

Finish the rectangle here.

6. Click on the select tool. Put your pointer above and left of the camel. Hold the left mouse button and drag out a rectangle.

7. Position your pointer over the camel. Holding the left mouse button down, drag the camel to the left of the screen. Let go of the mouse button.

8. Holding down the CTRL key on the keyboard, drag the camel to the right. It will leave a copy. Let go of the CTRL key and the mouse button.

9. Make more copies of the camel. Then, click on the paint can tool. Click on different colours and parts of the camels to colour them in.

Remember, if you make mistakes you can undo them. See pages 10-11 for how to do this.

Here, a background of sand dunes was drawn in behind the camel train.

You might only be able to fit three camels across your screen – it depends on the size of your screen and the camels.

Computer penguins

Using the computer program Paint, you can draw a group of animals by copying one animal again and again, and flipping some of the copies over to face the other way. See page 58 for how to open Paint, and pages 10 and 38 for how to use some of the tools you'll need.

A colony of penguins

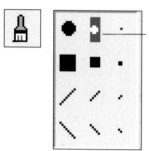

Click on this brush style.

1. Click on the black colour. Click on the brush tool. Below the tool box, click on the medium round brush style.

2. To draw, press the left mouse button and drag the mouse. Draw a head, a beak, a wing, a tail and a body.

3. Draw the other wing. Draw feet under the body. Add a line on the body. Click to make a dot for each eye.

Make sure there are no gaps in the outline.

4. Click on blue, then click on the paint can tool. Click on the penguin to colour it blue. Colour the belly pale yellow.

5. Click on orange in the paint box, and then click on the penguin's beak and feet to colour them orange.

6. Click on the select tool. Pressing the left mouse button down, drag a box around the penguin.

40

You could draw some smaller penguins in the scene, too.

Click on this option.

7. Click on the bottom option below the tool box. Pressing the CTRL key on the keyboard, drag the penguin to make a copy. Let the mouse button go.

8. Click on *Image* at the top of the screen. On the list that appears click on *Flip/Rotate*. In the box, click on *Flip horizontal*, and then on *OK*.

9. Copy and flip the penguin a few more times to make a whole colony. Use the brush and paint can tools to add icy hills in the background.

41

Head-on hippos

Animals look completely different shapes from the front than from the side. Front on, parts of an animal may be hidden by the rest of its body. Its body looks shorter than it actually is. This is called foreshortening.

Discover online

Scan the code to watch a video clip about hippos.

For more links, go to
www.usborne.com/quicklinks

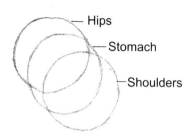

— Hips

— Stomach

— Shoulders

1. In pencil, draw three overlapping circles for the hips, stomach, and shoulders of a hippo.

2. Draw two circles in front for the head and nose. Add the eyes, nostrils and ears.

3. Draw front legs from the shoulder and a back leg from the hip.

4. Draw the outline, using the circles to show the fat body. Rub out the extra lines.

Leave a white highlight on one side.

Dab the pink on while the paint is damp.

5. Paint the hippo with brown watercolour, making one side darker than the other.

6. Add a little pink to the mouth and eyes. Let it dry. Draw the outline in fine felt-tip pen.

The grass was painted with green watercolour. When it was dry, the black lines were added using felt-tip.

The background was painted around the hippos before the outlines were added. See page 55 for how to do this.

Overlapping shapes

You can use the same shapes to draw a hippo from different angles. You need to overlap the circles more or less depending on which way the hippo is facing.

These body circles line up diagonally.

When drawing a hippo from behind, add a small tail.

These body circles spread out horizontally.

These body circles almost totally overlap.

Some yawning hippos were added to this scene, and the insides of their mouths painted pink.

Lines around the hippos show ripples in the water.

Wild horses

Horses can be quite tricky to draw. A good way of getting the proportions right is to compare the length of the animal's head with other parts of its body as you draw it. As you follow the steps below, try using the horse shown here to help you to get the shape right.

The blue lines on this horse are all the same length.

This shows how long different parts of the horse's body are compared to its head.

Discover online

Scan the code for a step-by-step lesson on how to draw a horse.

For more links, go to **www.usborne.com/quicklinks**

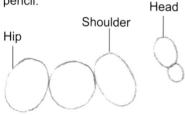

Draw this lightly in pencil.

Hip   Shoulder   Head

1. Draw a circle, with a slanted oval either side for the shoulder and hip. Draw two more ovals for the head.

The zigzags start from the centre of the ovals.

The hooves slope forwards.

2. Draw zigzag legs from the shoulder and the hip. Add circles for the joints. Then, add triangles for the hooves.

The back dips here.

The neck arches a bit.

3. Draw the outline around the shapes, like this. When you have finished, rub out any lines you don't need.

---

4. Add an ear pointing backwards. Rub out the part of the neck that overlaps it. Then, add the eye and nostril.

5. Draw two more zigzags for the other legs. Add hooves. Then, outline the legs and rub out the lines inside them.

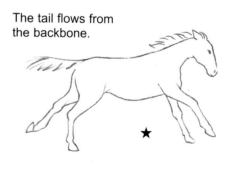

The tail flows from the backbone.

6. Draw the mane and tail using a few long lines. They are streaming out behind the horse to show its movement.

Fill in the far legs.

Paint under the body and neck.

Use the pencil line as a guide.

7. Mix some blue ink with lots of water to make a pale shade. Paint it in the places shown here to show the horse's shape.

8. Paint the pale blue in long, flowing lines to show the mane and the tail. The brush marks can go outside the lines.

9. When the horse is dry, go over the outline in blue pencil. Vary the pressure on the pencil to get thick and thin lines.

Blue ink was flicked from a paintbrush around the horses' feet to make it look like they are galloping through water.

The shadows beneath the horses' feet were added before the flicked ink.

Waxy zebras

Zebras are quite similar in shape to horses (see pages 44-45). When you look at a four-legged animal from an angle, the legs furthest from you look higher up or shorter. This is called perspective. You can use the technique shown here to draw horses or other four-legged animals from this angle.

Discover online

Scan the code to see lots of stripy zebras.

For more links, go to
www.usborne.com/quicklinks

These zebras were drawn in pencil, then filled in using white wax crayon and black ink.

The back looks like it goes upwards away from you.

★

The back legs look higher.

The grass below was drawn with wax crayon then yellow watercolour was painted on top.

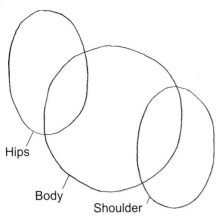

Hips

Body

Shoulder

1. In pencil, draw an oval for the hips, a circle overlapping it for the body, and another oval for the shoulder.

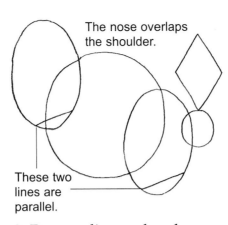

The nose overlaps the shoulder.

These two lines are parallel.

2. Draw a diamond and an oval for the head and nose. Draw two slanted lines inside the shoulder and hip ovals.

The vertical lines are parallel.

★

3. Draw four lines, one for each leg, coming from each end of the slanted lines. The lines for the legs should be parallel.

One knee looks higher than the other.

4. Draw a line parallel to the shoulder line, halfway down the front legs. Add the knees and then outline the legs.

5. Draw a line parallel to the hip line, halfway down the back legs. Add knee circles, and then outline the back legs.

★

6. Draw the rest of the outline. Add a tail. Then, rub out the extra shapes and lines inside the outline.

7. Add the ears, eyes and mane. With a thin, white wax crayon, put a dot in each eye for a highlight.

Colour these parts in white.

8. Add stripes, curving them around the body. Colour the white parts in wax crayon. Add white bits to the hooves.

If the ink sticks to the wax stripes, scrape it off with your fingernail.

9. Paint watered-down black ink all over the zebra's body. Most of it will run off the wax, letting the white parts show.

47

Kangaroos in motion

Animals are difficult to draw in motion but can make the most exciting pictures. If you draw an animal's legs using a zigzag line (see page 12), you can just change the shape of the zigzag to draw the legs in different positions.

The zigzag changes shape as the kangaroo moves.

Chalk pastels were used to draw these kangaroos.

The lines overlapping the outline give a sense of speed.

Press very lightly.

Press harder for the back and tail.

1. Draw a big oval and a smaller oval for the body. Add a circle for the head with a wedge-shaped muzzle.

2. Draw a curve for the back and the tail. Add a big zigzag for the back leg and a smaller one for the front leg.

3. Draw an outline around the head shapes. Add ears. Then, draw the rest of the outline, adding the legs and tail.

Lay a piece of scrap paper over the parts you have drawn to protect them, while you do the rest of your drawing.

You will need to fix this drawing so that it doesn't smudge. See page 59 for how.

Discover online

Scan the code to see how kangaroos move.

For more links, go to **www.usborne.com/quicklinks**

Your shading can go outside the outline a little.

Do all the lines in the same direction.

4. Use an orange chalk pastel to draw lots of lines all going in the same direciton. Leave some paper showing through.

5. Use a paler chalk pastel to add highlights on the kangaroo's back, tail, legs and on the head.

6. Use a darker chalk pastel to add the details to the face. Then, add shadows under the body, legs and tail.

Birds in flight

You can use the same basic shapes to draw birds in lots of different flight positions. Draw a seagull following the steps below. Then, use the flight positions section to help you draw more seagulls, and create a whole scene.

Add lines to show the bird's body.

1. In pencil, draw an oval body and a circle for a head. Draw lines to position the wings.

2. Add the wing shapes and draw the tail. Then, draw around the whole outline.

3. Rub out the extra lines inside the outline. Add the bird's eyes, the beak and feet.

Flight positions ★

When near the ground, a bird might drop its head and let its feet hang down.

When gliding, a bird straightens its wings and tucks in its feet.

When landing, a bird tilts its wings and drops its feet.

From the front, the body looks short and the wings look narrow.

Painting the scene

Leave the colour uneven to look like clouds.

1. Dampen the paper around the birds with a brush. Then, paint a blue watercolour sky.

2. When the sky is dry, use pale grey watercolour to paint shadows on the birds.

3. Use a little black watercolour to paint the eyes, and the tips of the wings and the tails.

4. Mix a bit of orange watercolour. Paint the beaks and feet of the birds. Let them dry.

Bird shapes

An eagle has very long, broad wings.

A swallow has angular wings and a forked tail.

A jay's body and wings are quite short.

You can draw different types of birds using very similar shapes to those used for drawing seagulls.

Discover online
Scan the code to watch birds flying in slow motion.

For more links, go to
www.usborne.com/quicklinks

Animals in action

As well as drawing animals in the poses shown throughout this book, you might want to draw them in other positions. You can use these drawings as reference to help you.

Eadweard Muybridge, an early photographer, took sequences of photographs like these to find out how animals move.

Dog ★

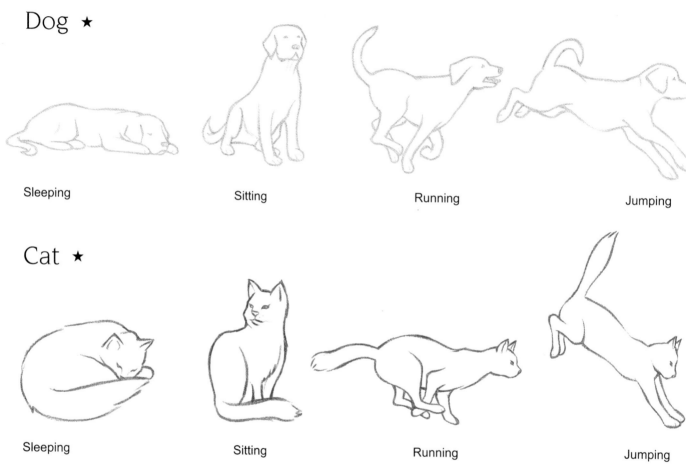

Sleeping

Sitting

Running

Jumping

Cat ★

Sleeping

Sitting

Running

Jumping

Rabbit ★

Grazing

Sitting up

Cleaning

Hopping

Discover online

Scan the code to watch a video of animals moving in slow motion.

For more links, go to **www.usborne.com/quicklinks**

Horse ★

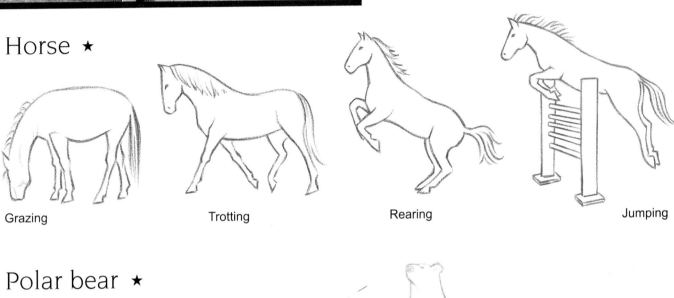

Grazing

Trotting

Rearing

Jumping

Polar bear ★

Sleeping

Walking

Rearing

Standing

Monkey ★

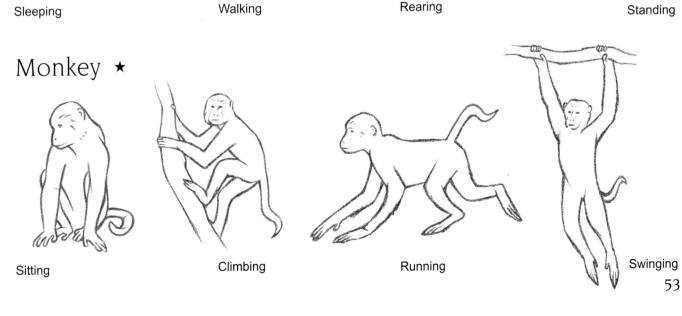

Sitting

Climbing

Running

Swinging

Animal environments

A background can add a lot to a drawing by showing where an animal is or emphasizing parts of its character. Here are some examples of the effect a choice of background can have on a picture, and tips on ways of painting backgrounds.

In this picture, the elephants' size is emphasized by their reflections in the water and by the trees behind them.

Horizon and scale

The size you draw an animal in relation to its background can make it look bigger or smaller. You can also use the horizon line (where the land and sky meet) to emphasize an animal's size.

This bear is bursting out of its background. The horizon line is very low. This makes the bear look huge.

This bear family is tiny against the hills. The horizon line is high, making the bears look like just a small part of their environment.

Painting a background first

1. Paint a pale watercolour wash for the background (see page 34). Leave it until it is completely dry.

2. Add an animal in a stronger colour. The background colour will show through, so it's best to use similar colours on top.

You could add details in coloured pencil once the paint is dry.

Painting an animal first

1. Paint an animal. Let it dry. Then, paint clean water onto the background, right up to the edges of the animal.

2. Paint a colour wash around the animal. Don't go right up to the outline: the damp paper will carry the colour up to it.

You could add an outline when it is dry, or it might look good without one.

Painting around an animal

Paint the details on top with a fine brush.

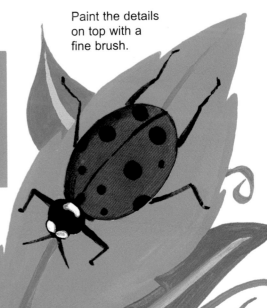

1. Draw outlines for the whole scene. Paint the background areas, overlapping the outline of the animal very slightly.

2. When the background is dry, paint the animal so that its outline overlaps the background a little.

Drawing from life

Animals are difficult to draw from life, as you can't ask them to sit still. Drawing animals you see around you is the ideal way to learn how to draw them. So, here are a few tips to help you.

David Hockney's drawing of his dogs 'Stanley and Boodgie 23 September 93' was one of many sketches and paintings he made of them.

Drawing sleepy pets

If you have a pet, then you can practise drawing it again and again. A good time to draw animals is when they are asleep because they will be staying quite still.

1. Draw some simple shapes and a rough outline of the animal's pose, first.

2. Add more detail to the outline once you have drawn the whole shape.

3. If the animal moves, you can still look at details, like its whiskers, and draw them.

Feeding time

If you visit a farm or zoo, you can draw the animals in their enclosures. Try drawing them at feeding time, when they are more likely to be all in one place and not moving around too much.

Animals that are eating tend to repeat certain movements again and again.

When drawing from life, look at the animal before you draw each line on your page. This will make your drawing more accurate.

Drawing groups

When drawing a group of animals, look at different animals in the group to catch their poses. If there's a whole group of ducks for example, you can look at lots of different birds to draw one, as they will all repeat the same poses.

Draw the animals in the front larger and with more detail than the ones in the background. Also, make the background ones paler.

Materials for drawing

What you choose to draw with and to draw on will have an effect on how your drawing looks. These pages tells you a little about materials and what effects you can get.

Discover online

Scan the code to find out about different techniques and materials.

For more links, go to
www.usborne.com/quicklinks

How to open Microsoft® Paint

The computer drawing program, Paint, can be found on any computer with Microsoft® Windows®. Here's how to open it.

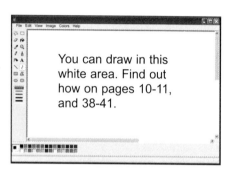

You can draw in this white area. Find out how on pages 10-11, and 38-41.

1. Move your pointer over *Start*. Click with the left mouse button. A list will appear on your screen.

2. Move the pointer up the list to *Programs* and click. Another list will appear. Move across to *Accessories* and click.

3. On the list that appears, move the pointer to *Paint* and click. The Paint window will appear on your screen.

Paintbrushes

You can get lots of different kinds of paintbrushes which are good for different things. Soft paintbrushes (sable or synthetic) are good for using watercolours or inks. More coarsely textured brushes are good with acrylic paints.

Thick brushes are good for filling in large areas of colour.

Fine brushes are good for details or outlines.

Always rinse your brushes well after painting. Leaving paint on them will damage the bristles.

Pencils

Pencils come in different levels of hardness or softness. They are labelled with a number and a letter – either B (meaning soft) or H (meaning hard). The higher the number, the harder or softer the pencil. For example, 9B is very soft and 9H is very hard. HB is medium.

Soft pencils make dark, blurry lines and are good for drawing varied textures and bold images.

Hard pencils make light, thin lines and are good for drawing delicate detail.

Papers

You can use good quality cartridge paper for most things, but different types of paper are good for using with particular materials. Here are some examples.

Pastels look good on textured pastel paper. The colours look bright and blend well on the paper.

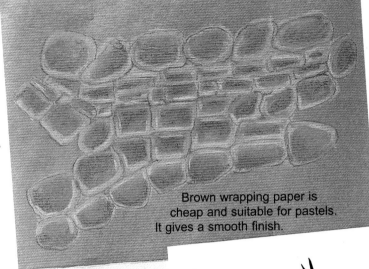

Brown wrapping paper is cheap and suitable for pastels. It gives a smooth finish.

Rough watercolour paper gives your drawings texture.

Smooth, or hotpress, watercolour paper gives a sleek finish.

Printing computer pictures onto coloured paper will alter the colours.

Acrylic paints work well on thick paper or cardboard.

Fixing drawings

If you use soft pencils or chalk pastels you should fix your drawing so it doesn't smudge. You can do this by spraying it with fixative spray or hairspray. Always follow the directions on the can, and fix pictures outside or somewhere with lots of fresh air.

Spray in sweeping movements going horizontally and then vertically.

Don't use too much spray.

Gallery

Over the next four pages you can see a gallery of animal pictures, which were drawn or painted using techniques and materials described in this book. Look through the gallery for new ideas. You can turn back to the pages mentioned to read more about certain techniques.

These three animals were drawn and painted using inks.

This penguin scene was painted in watercolours using a similar technique to the dolphin scene on pages 34-35.

This gorilla was drawn in chalk pastels, like the orangutan on page 23, but using a more realistic style.

This racoon was drawn in felt-tip pen. Then, the lines were smudged with a wet paintbrush (see page 17).

Discover online

Scan the code to find out about an artist who paints animals.

For more links, go to
www.usborne.com/quicklinks

This bird's head was drawn from a photograph using pencil. The shading technique is similar to that described on page 14.

This frog was painted in watercolours. The colours were blended on wet paper, in a similar way to the dolphins' bodies on page 35.

This toucan was drawn on computer in Microsoft® Paint using shape tools and the brush tool (see pages 10 and 38).

This cat was drawn and shaded in pencil, in a similar way to the dog on page 9 and the mouse on page 16.

Discover online

Scan the code to watch a video clip about an artist who paints animals.

For more links, go to **www.usborne.com/quicklinks**

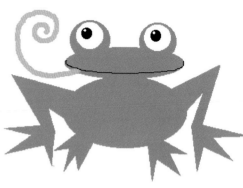

This frog was drawn on a computer using Microsoft® Paint (see pages 10 and 38).

This pig was drawn quickly using felt-tip pen. Then, the lines were smudged with a wet paintbrush (see page 17).

This chicken was painted from life with coloured inks and a small brush.

These crocodiles were painted in watercolour, then outlined in felt-tip pen. The same technique was used for the hippos on pages 42-43.

This tiger was drawn in a cartoony style using watercolour and fine felt-tip pen.

This chameleon was painted using watercolours. The colours on the body were painted on wet paper to make them blend together (see page 32).

This cow was drawn from life using white, brown and black conté crayons (which are similar to chalk pastels, see pages 20-23).

Index

Acknowledgements

Every effort has been made to trace the copyright holders of the material in this book. If any rights have been omitted, the publishers offer their sincere apologies and will rectify this in any subsequent editions following notification. The publishers are grateful to the following organizations and individuals for their contributions and permission to reproduce material:

Page 4 Elephant painting © Earl & Nazima Kowall/CORBIS
Page 5 Rhinoceros by Albrecht Dürer © Bettmann/CORBIS; Adonis, King George III's Favourite Charger by James Ward, © Christie's Images/CORBIS
Page 6 Wet Red Fox Along Green Grass © Joe McDonald/CORBIS
Page 8 Leopard, rhinoceros, penguin, marmot, antelope © Digital Vision
Page 12 Pisanello, Antonio Pucci (or Pucino) 'Deux Vaches et une Génisse Couches' aka 'Three Cows' (detail) c. 1430-1440. Silver point, pencil and pen © RMN/Thierry Le Mage
Page 16 Albrecht Dürer, 'The Young Hare' 1502, Watercolour and gouache on paper © SuperStock, Inc./SuperStock
Page 18 Roosters by Ito Jakuchu, © Sakamoto Photo Research Laboratory/CORBIS
Page 28 Henri Rousseau 'Tiger in a Tropical Storm (Surprised!)' 1891.

Oil on canvas © The National Gallery, London
Page 37 Edward Lear cat drawings 'Nonsense Songs and Stories', (pp. 138-141), 1894. Reference (shelfmark) Opie PP 583 © Bodleian Library, University of Oxford
Page 52 Eadweard Muybridge horse photographs. Plate 626 © Kingston Museum and Heritage Service
Page 54 Elephants © Digital Vision
Page 56 David Hockney 'Stanley and Boodgie 23 September 93' 1993. Crayon on paper. 22 1/2 x 30 1/4 © David Hockney
Page 57 Koala © Tom Brakefield/CORBIS
Microsoft product screen shots on pages 10-11, 38-41, and 58 reprinted with permission from Microsoft Corporation. Microsoft®, Microsoft® Windows® 2000 and Microsoft® Paint are either registered Trade Marks or Trade Marks of Microsoft Corporation in the US and other countries.

Picture researcher: Ruth King. Thanks to R. Phillips, Gillian Doherty and Brenda Gladding for providing animal photographs.